A Poem Keeps the Teachers Away

Daisy Harris

A Poem a Day Keeps the Teachers Away ©
2023 Daisy Harris

All rights reserved.

No part of this publication may be reproduced, stored in a retrieval system, or transmitted, in any form or by any means, electronic, mechanical, photocopying, recording or otherwise, without the prior written permission of the presenters.

Daisy Harris asserts the moral right to be identified as author of this work.

Presentation by *BookLeaf Publishing*

Web: www.bookleafpub.com

E-mail: info@bookleafpub.com

ISBN: 9789357440486

First edition 2023

*I hereby dedicate this book to my parents,
who tried*

ACKNOWLEDGEMENT

First and foremost, I must thank Netflix for keeping me sane - no easy feat mind you.

I must also acknowledge the contents of my snack cupboard, especially crisps, which stood by me and sacrificed themselves for my enjoyment.

I guess Samson Newman could be thanked, I mean he dealt with my obsession with this book and he donated one line (the one about the leprechaun).

Izzy Buckley is the best and helps me with literally everything. She seemed to be the only one who didn't get fed up with me about this book!

My poor poor teachers need a mention as well for dealing with me for all these years.

Olive and Jacob, mi siblanos, now you have your names in a book.

PREFACE

I would like to begin by confessing that I'm not entirely sure what a preface is. I asked google, and apparently it's like a behind the scenes, but for books.

Sounds a bit boring so I think I'll skip it.

Sorry

Mars

Red is normally a warning…
Danger! Stay away
Is Mars warning us?
Or simply saying stop.
Don't come to this planet.

Like how a tree frog
Sports bright colours
To ward of predators

Maybe, Mars is fighting back

Mars doesn't want to perish
It doesn't want the same fate
The same torture it watched
It's neighbour destroyed
By a selfish species
Inhumane, insatiable, iniquitous

Now we move to Mars
The red planet
But what if Mars doesn't want us?

Knowing

Mouth parched
Licking cracked lips
With a tongue roughed
The addiction grips

So thirsty for knowledge
Consuming every hour
Everyone acknowledge
The higher power

Superiority in knowing
Intelligence and wisdom
Need possessing
For this corrupted system

I am in the know
But that's not always
Worth the show
Worth the praise

It's eating me up inside
Secrets, stories
Absorbed wide-eyed
Exciting discoveries

Knowing should never
Cause regret or sadness
So should I endeavour
To fix mistakes from predecessors

Stooped under the weight
Having too much
Behind the gates
No one can touch

Fragile, delicate, breakable
Tiptoe around
My fear unmistakable
So be gentle… don't make a sound

Secrets strain
Liberty in their heart
Endless pain
Pulling me apart

Unrecognisable to me
Knowledge's power
Absolute over me
Looming over every hour

Knowledge is dangerous
In the wrong hands
Or it could save us
From our own commands

Knowing is a gift
Intelligence and wisdom
Causes a rift
In our system

You can't return
What was given to you
Even if you burn
From what you knew

I can never go back
To blissful ignorance
Unfortunate drawback
From my perseverance

"Ignorance is bliss"
"Knowledge is power"
Pick from this
Which be your superpower?

I picked wrong
Pick yours right
Or your tongue
Will be as dry as mine

Toll

Acting strong as if I don't
Care what he thinks about
Me because it hurts too
Much to think about how
He doesn't feel the same
Way about me because
He is a clueless boy who
Doesn't understand my feelings

Every day I put up this
Weighty facade which over
Time has placed a toll on
My sensitive heart which
Beats only for him but he
Can't hear how fast my heart
Is beating for him because he
Doesn't understand my feelings

Maybe one day he might find
Something in his cold heart which
Doesn't beat for me as mine
Does for him and this takes a
Toll on me and my heart which
Grows weaker with every beat
For him because he still

Doesn't understand my feelings

As my heart fades away into
Nothingness I wonder whether he
Might have loved me too but
He was too shy to say too
Scared to talk to me and to
Tell me how when he couldn't
Hear my beating heart he
Didn't understand my feelings

Because he wanted to tell me
How his heart beats just
A little faster when we are
Together like mine does when
He looks at me from across
The crowded room and our
Eyes meet I try to tell him how
To understand my feelings

But everything was lost because
The toll on my heart became
Too much for me and I
Couldn't put up the brave
Face anymore because I
Had loved him for too long
Without thinking that it was I who
Didn't understand HIS feelings

Temptation

The pull is undeniable
It's almost magnetic
The end is inevitable
And I'm not apologetic

But can I resist it?
Desire overpowers me
My stomach a deep pit
Please, set me free!

It's been so long
The craving is relentless
Can I stay strong
This torture is endless

Unless… the end is nigh
It's time to give in
Something I can't dignify
Committing this final sin

So I must open the packet
Submit to my desires

And eat the crisps.

Verano

Sun beats down on my skin
Waves splashing
Children playing, ocupados
Sand warm against me
Lying with him
En un verano bonito
Con el
Soy feliz con el
Me encanta el verano
I can be with him
All day
All night
My life is on pause por seis semanas
I'm free from responsibility
Free from pressure
On la playa
Con el
En verano

Mistake

You had all the power
Holding a loaded gun
I was left to cower
You shot me for fun

Now I'm bleeding
Bleeding on the floor
You were so misleading
I'm optimistic no more

My heart fades away
But you don't care
I wanted you to stay
But you weren't there

You abandoned me
When I needed you most
Now you are all I see
Haunted by your ghost

Your fake security
Offers of love and care
Dressed up all pretty
Now laid out bare

You can't hide anything
Something I won't allow
Don't use me as a plaything
You can't trick me now

I made my mistake
I thought you were the one
But you were just a fake
Now that you are gone

You thought you were clever
I don't need you anymore
So goodbye forever
Our love is no more

Rainbow

Follow the rainbow to the end
Run down it's multicoloured road
Chase round every bend
Wonder consumed, eyes glowed
Wishes and dreams can come true
When you look outside your window
And a leprechaun looks at you
Get to the end of the rainbow
Find a world of pure delight
Spend a day in heaven
Bask in its kaleidoscope of light
Ah, the joys of being eleven

But remember the stories of old
And if you find that pot of gold
A gift for all to behold...
But a promise you must uphold

You have to be home by five for tea

Don't Turn the Light Off

Don't turn the light off
I need my night light
The bright stars help me
Sleep through the night
Singing songs of youth

Don't turn the light off
My heart aches to find
Someone who can love me
Under the light intertwined
Singing songs of adolescence

Don't turn the light off
Then I can't find my glasses
They hide away from me
Then the night passes
Singing songs of lost time

Don't turn the light off
The night is dark
Tall trees terrify me
With wrinkled crinkled bark
Singing songs of old age

Don't turn the light off
The end is near
What will happen to me
Without the light I fear
The song of death

Mind Demon

Lurking deep, hidden
Amongst the hullabaloo
Stalking.
Corrupted ideas roaming
In the darkest depths
Feeding the hunger
Keeping me
Awake
All
The
Time
I can't sleep with her
Creeping, crawling, crowding
Around my thoughts
Polluting them,
Making my life miserable
I'm always tired
Whilst she is looming over
My vulnerable mind
Causing internal struggles, conflicts, arguments, wars
Why is she there?
Leave me alone!
I
Want

To
Sleep.
Alien thoughts begin to gently ease my conscience
Into things I would never do
Scaring me
Confusing me
Making her presence even more prominent
I should feel guilty
But it's not my fault!
Why won't she leave me alone
My evil mind demon
Wreaking havoc

Lift Off

Ten years staring at your face
Wishing it was mine
You've always had a special place
Here in my heart

Nine nights you poisoned my dreams
With your dreamy eyes
I can't get you out of my mind
You are all I think about

Eight times I've tried to talk to you
To tell you how I feel
But I don't want to lose you forever
Is it a risk I'm willing to take?

Seven days until the holidays
Surely I can say something
I can't miss my chance
Or I will always wonder: what if?

Six sidewards glances I received
Your cheeky smirk
Do you know what you are doing to me?
Maybe it's intentional

Five minutes of awkwardness
Why did I tell you?
Now I fear I've ruined everything
My bravely now seemingly foolish

Four hours of messaging that night
Were you too scared to admit your feelings?
I thought you didn't want me
But now I'm filled with hope

Three words: I like you
Opened doors to our future
I want to explore this new world
But only with you

Two weeks without you, how will I cope?
I miss you already
I'm finally happy
I don't want to leave you

One last kiss before I set off
Our final goodbyes are done
But our relationship has just lifted off
The adventure is yet to come

Divorce

Prancing around, proud, arrogant
After destroying OUR family
Ripping up OUR foundations
Hoping the house doesn't collapse

But it did, when HE left
Because HE left ME
Why did HE think HE had the audacity
To leave ME

Having to manage on my own
It's different, it's lonely
Without him
Why can't I seem to live without him?

Walking away seemed easy for HIM
Like HE didn't care about US
Always selfish, always uncaring
Oblivious to the world around HIM

HE was thoughtless
HE couldn't see how this could effect ME
And HE was happy to hurt ME
His cold heart easily left ME

Despite his self-centred ways
I loved HIM
However misguided
So why did HE leave ME?

I was good to HIM
Gave HIM everything HE ever wanted
I didn't know HE was capable of this cruelty
Making ME ashamed

Why should I have to feel guilty
HE did this to ME
HE destroyed US
HE divorced ME

Shadows

Whispering softly in my ear
Shivering in anticipation
Telling me I have nothing to fear
I am safe when he is near

Even if he isn't here, his
Shadows crawl across my body
Ghost of lips, our first kiss
Something I dearly miss

Memories saved into my skin
Stories waiting to be told
Lurking shadows of the sin
Delusions start to spin

My mind creating, manifesting
Hopeful futures yet to unfold
Shadows' stories completing
Images begin repeating

I always want him near me
Branded into me, living memory
Like tattoos no one can see
Everyone except he

He can see the damage done
Whenever he looks in my eyes
Tarnished by our past fun
Scarred by futures yet to come

Daydream

Sun dazed, sleepy and distracted
Bout of daydream been contracted
Off flying in a strange new realm
My crazy mind at the helm

Sometimes life can be so boring
So new worlds need exploring
In my mind I can do anything
A kingdom where I am king

Daydreams can lead to revelations
In this word without regulations
You can learn who you truly are
When you mind is lost afar

And when you awaken, confused
You may have to be excused
As you weren't paying attention
So you will end up in detention!

Ghosts

Pale hazel haunting
Shadow behind my eyes
Always there, lurking
A simple compromise

Soft whispers echo
Distracting me too
Showing me the window
Back to you

Should I travel
Ghosts I follow
Story yet to unravel
Empty and hollow

Now you chase me
Silently amongst stones
It's you I can't see
Hiding behind their bones

Should I choose this
Or let you go?
Stay for a last kiss…
Or free the crow?

Vines

Your hurtful words cracking
Our foundations breaking,
Tearing falling apart
Destroying our love

They slither out between
Newfound cracks and breaks
Slimy vines climbing, covering
Your nasty words dominating

You've trapped me.
And you're proud of your work
In love with your hurtful
Cruel caging circle

There is no escape
Vines holding me captive
So you can watch me cry
Revelling in my pain

Why have you forsaken me so?
I deserve better
So I will free myself
From your possessive vines

Silence

Holding my breath, underneath
Silence surrounding, consuming
Water protecting me beneath
Noise, bustle, rushing, raging

Enclosed in her watery embrace
I'm free from everything, everyone
Always safe, my favourite place
No one around, never anyone

So silent, peaceful, alone with you
Underneath the waves together
In the silent, murky blue
Locked away together forever

Soothing silence washes over me
Willing me to take my last breath
We will be together, at last free
Silence found long in my death

Golgotha

Wind blows brisk across
Eyes watering, heaving
The heavy, heavy cross
Are you there father?

Throngs come storming,
Striding - just to see
My inevitable execution.
Where are you father?

Slowly approaching now
The begging of the end
Thorn halo, crown of death
Father? Father?

Oh how ignorance and hate
Lead to fear and paranoia
I will forgive them but
I need your strength father!

Death lays anticipating
Nearing, his breath lurks
Behind my ear whispering:

Your father isn't coming to save you…

Talking

You never lie to me
When you are sleeping
Words spout without thought
Your truth between snores

You talk to me
When you are asleep
I learn all your secrets
Everything you keep from me

Guilt ridden lies
Names I don't know
What is this secret life
You dream about every night

It spills from your mouth
Like a song yet to be sung
Chorus tripping off your tongue
Our trust now undone

Let loose your inhibitions
As sleep overtakes you
You will never lie to me
When you talk in your sleep

Olympus

Zealots swarm after their King
Eager just for a glimpse
Undying praise on their lips
Swearing their eternal love

Powerful and mighty sea
Ominous waves threaten
Sailors pray to their god
Ever present underwater
Idolised by sea farers
Dominating their waters
Overshadowing their choices
Never letting go

Hiding in the underworld
A secret life he leads
Death is the only door
Enemies beware
Sometimes evil is good…

Gently

Stillwater surrounds us
So we row carefully
Gliding across the lake
Gently
His smile in the blue
Glows in the sun
I watch him row
Gently
His hands on the oar
Moving with ease
I watch his hair
Gently
Blows in the wind
Brushing softly
I watch his eyes
Gently
Gazing at the horizon
Wondering, pondering
He watches me
Gently
Sweat dripping down
Sun's sweltering heat
He watches my oar
Gently
Dipping in and out

Disrupting the calm
He watches my feet
Gently
Bouncing up and down
Nerves showing
Rocking the boat
Gently!
Don't rock the boat.

Closed

Towering above, mocking me
Walls you built up around yourself
To protect you
Why?

Why don't you trust anyone?
You can trust me
I won't hurt your delicate soul
Like so many have done

Isolated from all emotions
No love passes through your walls
You are closed off from the world
Closed off from me

How do I show you that you can trust me?
I want to pass through those walls
I want to know you
Why won't you let me?

Instead I have to peer through the cracks
Hoping for a glimpse
Hoping for a shimmer of your beautiful blue
eyes
Hoping you aren't lost forever

I care about you
More than I would like to admit
So please let me in
So I can show you how much I care
So I can show you love
So I can show you me

Ingram Content Group UK Ltd.
Milton Keynes UK
UKHW021418040723
424531UK00015B/680